Who Is Piperoo?

How do you say Piperoo?
It's a name that rhymes with kangaroo.
Three pipe cleaners, red, yellow and blue.
Say it slowly pipe - a - roo.

Piperoo loves to tell us
of beautiful things all around.
Piperoo loves to share with us all
the wonderful things to be found.
Piperoo travels all over the place.
Piperoo even travels through space.

Piperoo learns something every day.
Creatures that swim in the sea.
Different countries and different animals.
How The Earth came to be.
Adding up and taking away,
what to eat and words to say.

Piperoo loves to share with you
each discovery.
Piperoo loves to teach you big words
like mathematics and geography.
So many things Piperoo wishes to do
and Piperoo wishes to share them with you.

Piperoo has so many stories to tell,
so many great things to share.
Places and faces around the world.
Piperoo takes us all there.
Piperoo is here for me and you,
a chance for us all to learn something new.

ENGLISH

Words like climb, lime and time
are very clever words that rhyme.
Think, blink and now you see
that's what's known as poetry.

Piperoo's Little Words

When a word is very young,
its letters number perhaps just one.
Like I and A and then it's two,
like me, my, go and do.
Then cat and dog add up to three.
That's how a big word comes to be.

Sh is a very small, two letter word.
It means that nothing should be heard.
If you add the letter E
Sh becomes she, now you see.

At the end of she you add a D
A four-letter word comes to be.
Not three letters, four instead.
She has now turned into shed.

Six is heaven, Dolphin is seven,
then words grow as big as ten and eleven.
Such words are too big for you and me,
but that's how big words come to be.

Piperoo's Types of Words

A verb is a doing word,
often used and often heard.
To swim or walk along the kerb,
every action is a verb.

Another word to learn is noun.
It means a name or perhaps a town.
So a noun is what we call your name.
Where you live is just the same.

A big word you must now forgive.
This word is called an adjective.
It describes a word and comes before it,
a drink is a yummy drink as you pour it.

A wonderful day is just a day
if you take the adjective away
Without nouns your name would disappear,
so just be happy nouns are here.

The Piperoo Wants Poem

Piperoo wants to play hockey.
Piperoo wants to be a jockey.
Piperoo wants to dance like a baboon.
Piperoo wants to fly like a balloon.
Piperoo wants to ride a bicycle.
Piperoo wants to hang like an icicle.
Piperoo wants to open a parcel.
Piperoo wants to build a sandcastle.
Piperoo wants to jump like a frog.
Piperoo wants to walk like a dog.
Piperoo wants to be in a play.
Piperoo wants to see a firework display.
Piperoo wants to help bake a cake.
Piperoo wants to crawl like a snake.
Piperoo wants to swim in a pool.
Piperoo wants to bounce like a ball.
Piperoo wants to share with you.
All the things Piperoo wants to do.

FOOD

Think of food,
the more the better,
but only starting
with a Piperoo letter.

Piperoo Food

Peas, ice-cream, pasta and eggs,
give strength to Piperoo's arms and legs.
Rice, oats and oranges too
are healthy foods that spell Piperoo.

Another thing you should know
is that vitamins help you grow.
For Vitamin B eat lots of greens,
bananas, milk and all kinds of beans.

Vitamin E your body needs.
Vitamin E comes with sunflower seeds.
Nuts are also good for Vitamin E.
Mushrooms and fish give you Vitamin D.

A Piperoo poem to let you know
of the healthy food to help you grow.
Using Piperoo's letters try yourself
to find more food good for your health.

How Food Came To Be

Mother Nature made flowers with petals.
On a bad day she made stinging nettles.
Daffodils were her dancing gems,
she designed them all and put them on stems.

She placed the flowers wherever she could,
some in meadows, bluebells in a wood.
Beautiful colours, yellows and reds,
then along came vegetable beds.

And in those vegetable beds grew peas,
Beside them grew the bean
And so they were different to flowers
she painted each vegetable green.

Broccoli, peppers cabbages,
cauliflowers and leeks were seen
And just in case you have your doubts,
she also invented Brussels sprouts.

So now you know why you've never seen
a single flower that's painted green.

MATHEMATICS

Although it is tricky for everyone,
Mathematics can be fun.
You start by counting one, two, three,
the number of letters in a bee.

Count on Piperoo

Piperoo is flying in search of a horse.
How many is Piperoo looking for?
One of course!
If that horse has a special friend like you,
there wouldn't be just one horse,
there would be ?
Two.

Now Piperoo is searching for a tree.
Piperoo's found not one, not two, but three.
If clever Piperoo found one more,
how many trees would Piperoo find?
Four.

Count to five using your hand.
As Piperoo flies to a different land.
Six elephants are about to run.
So count from six down to one.

Piperoo's Take-Away

Piperoo loves eating cakes
Just like I'm sure you do
If Piperoo had three cakes and ate one
There wouldn't be three cakes but two

Piperoo then had two cakes
Both of them Piperoo ate
Now there are no cakes for Piperoo to eat
Just an empty plate

Piperoo had eaten them all
Because Piperoo so loved cake
Piperoo was left with nothing at all
apart from a tummy ache.

NATURE

Nature is a beautiful word
that tells us of all living things.
All that lives here, not just us,
but those with fins, whiskers and wings.

Piperoo Goes Swimming

Piperoo is going swimming today.
Piperoo's swimming underwater.
There are five oceans on The Earth,
some are deeper, some are shorter.

The largest is The Pacific.
then next comes The Atlantic.
Compared to the other three
these two are gigantic.

So what are the other three?
The Indian, Southern and Arctic.
To swim The Arctic Piperoo must be bold.
There are polar bears and it's very cold.

Piperoo is swimming and looking around.
Let us see what Piperoo has found.
The biggest is the huge blue whale,
with great big head and great big tale.

Also there are little crabs
and other things like shrimps and dabs.
A dab is called a flatfish
A whale isn't, that's a fat fish.

They all go wherever they please
in the five oceans and the seven seas.
Piperoo sees a turtle swimming along,
it swims alongside and then it has gone.

So many fish of so many sizes,
to capture food some have disguises.
So many colours under the sea,
so many fish that Piperoo can see

Piperoo waves to creature that pass.
proud sea horse and dolphin so fast.
A tear comes to Piperoo's eye
as a friendly turtle waves goodbye.

Piperoo's Nature Facts

Did you know a whale can talk
And hummingbirds cannot walk?
A bird must reach 11mph to fly
and pigs cannot look up to the sky.

An albatross goes to sleep as it flies,
An ostrich's brain is not as big as its eyes.
It takes 40 minutes to boil an ostrich egg.
A flamingo always stands on its left leg.

Hippos can't swim, they walk in the mud.
Did you know a lobster has blue blood?
A bat turns left when it leaves its house.
A panda at birth is the size of a mouse.

Blue whales are The World's biggest mammals.
Giraffes live without water longer than camels.
A tiger can grow over 3 metres long.
Piperoo's nature facts go on and on.

Piperoo Meets An Otter

Piperoo today will teach us
that rats and otters are two different creatures.
The beautiful creature, the otter
thinks the rat is a rotter.
It's because they both look the same,
which leads to the otter's great pain

Otters swim with their nose,
unlike a rat it doesn't have toes.
An otter has long, webbed feet
and it keeps its fur clean and neat.
So it isn't surprising the otter
thinks the rat is a rotter.
They're different and Piperoo's shown how
So we all know the difference now.

GEOGRAPHY

Places and countries, their rivers and streams
are what the big word Geography means.
Places to and countries to see
are found by that big word Geography.

Piperoo Visits Countries

Waterfalls are nature's taps
It is hard to see them marked on maps.
In case your searching is a failure
The highest waterfall is in Venezuela

Angel Falls drops from the sky.
It is around 900 metres high.
it is fifteen times higher than Niagara Falls
the most famous of our waterfalls

Russia is the biggest country on Earth,
six million square miles for what it is worth.
Then comes Canada and The United States,
these three are the all-time greats.

And yet as big as these countries may be,
two-thirds of our planet is covered by sea.
From the sea come rivers, mile upon mile,
the longest of which is The River Nile.

In most of our countries, rivers are found.
They start out as leaks springing out of the ground.
Then they grow bigger, just like you and me
as they journey along in search of the sea.

All Around The World

All around the world
there are places where Piperoo's been.
All around the world
there are places Piperoo's seen.
Big ones with deserts,
little ones with lakes.
Cold ones with polar bears
and scary ones with snakes.
All around the world
are places Piperoo's been.

All around the world
are people Piperoo's seen.
All around the world
are people where Piperoo's been.
They gave him a smile
Some give him a wave.
Some get close to Piperoo
Because they're very brave
All around the world
are people Piperoo's seen.

Children of the world
Each with a different name
Children of the world

inside are all the same
Some live in Britain.
Some live in Japan.
Some live in China
and some live in Iran.
Children of the world
inside are all the same.

All around the world
there are places where Piperoo's been.
All around the world
there are places Piperoo's seen.
Big ones with deserts,
little ones with lakes.
Cold ones with polar bears
and scary ones with snakes.
All around the world
are places Piperoo's been.

SCIENCE

Stories of space and life on Earth.
How we got here, our Planet's birth.
The air we breathe and how we live
are secrets the subject of Science will give.

Piperoo In Space

Piperoo is about to journey through space,
through distant stars to a distant place.
Millions and millions of miles away,
that's where Piperoo is flying today.

Piperoo is flying up in the sky,
through the stars above our heads.
A million trillion bedside lights
for a million trillion beds.

If The Sun was a juicy orange,
way up in the tallest tree,
then Planet Earth would be the size
of a little garden pea.

Did you know The Sun's so great
a million elephants are an equal weight?
It doesn't really go in, not at all,
it's always there, a bright blazing ball.

The hardest thing to learn by far?
Names of the planets and where they are.
Venus is different to all the rest
as it spins around from east to west.

One more fact, for what it's worth,
Venus is the same size as Planet Earth.
Saturn's rings look sparkling and nice.
Made up of millions of pieces of ice.

Saturn's winds have incredible power,
They travel at 1,000 miles per hour.
The sunlight that brings us smiles
has travelled 93 million miles.

Just to give you some idea,
8 minutes it takes from The Sun to here.
Jupiter is the largest without a doubt.
Bigger than Saturn we just learnt about

Uranus, Neptune and Earth the next three,
then Venus, Mars and Mercury.
Piperoo has taken us into space,
through twinkling stars to a distant place.

Life On Earth

Two thousand million years ago
a plant called algae began to show.
It was algae growing way back then
that started forming oxygen.

Twenty-three per cent of air,
that is oxygen's percentage share,
produced by plants beneath the sun,
breathing space for everyone.

Before oxygen the earth was a mass,
a great big ball of swirling gas.
Nitrogen and hydrogen too,
then water started seeping through.

Oxygen then was soon breathed in
through flowers, showers and things with skin.
We all breathe it into our lungs,
then out carbon dioxide comes.

So every creature big or small
now must answer to the call.
It can't be rocket science can it?
We must do our best to save the planet.

Piperoo in the Snow

Warm air rises high and proud.
It cools to ice and becomes a cloud.
The water then falls down as rain.
and empty clouds fill up again.

Sometimes it falls to us below
as frozen water known as snow.
No snowflake's shape is the same,
so each snowflake could have a name.

Frosty or Sparkle are just two,
many more wait to be named by you.
Warm air rises high and proud.
It cools to ice and forms another cloud.

Piperoo built a snowman one day,
out came The Sun and it melted away.
Piperoo acted like a clown
and ended up in the snow, upside down

HISTORY

Historic things are very old.
Made up of ancient stories told.
How we and our planet came to be.
That's what they call History.

What Is History?

Whatever happened, what came to be
Is known as one word, history
History tells us through the years,
what comes along and disappears.

Twenty-five thousand years ago
the Ice Age brought us freezing snow.
That's when snowmen first appeared.
In those days each had a big long beard.

And when that Ice Age came along
Planet Earth had much more water.
The North and South Poles had icebergs…
Some were tall and some were shorter.

Planet Earth had just begun
warming up beneath the Sun.
Spinning round and round in space,
a dusty, rusty coloured place.

There were no rivers, no tall trees.
No pretty flowers in the breeze.
Not green and blue as it is today,
that was millions of years away.

Little weeds were first to sprout,
then great big trees their heads popped out.
Yes trees were sprouting everywhere
with great big heads and leafy hair.

The world became an exciting place
As more animals began to appear.
Elephants, leopards, sheep with shepherds
And the forests filled with red deer.

So suddenly there were noises
as animals began to speak
Some of their voices were really loud.
Others just gave a small squeak.

Castles

Castles are found all over the world.
They are found in fairytales too.
Most are made of very old stones,
but some are pink, grey or blue

Some were built beside beautiful lakes.
Some were built on high,
upon the tops of grassy hills,
reaching way into the sky.

Some were homes of kings and queens,
guarded by soldiers so grand
but the greatest castles in the world
are built by children with sand.

Old castles stand for hundreds of years.
You can still see them today.
A sandcastle only stays a short time
until the sea comes to wash it away.

Sandcastles have so many stories
and so many games to be played.
Built through the dreams of children,
with the help of a bucket and spade.

Piperoo Bonus

Piperoo Says

Piperoo says gulp like a goldfish.
Piperoo says hiss like a snake.
Piperoo says growl like a tiger.
Blow bubbles like a fish in a lake.
Piperoo says snort like a piggy.
Piperoo says cluck like a hen.
Everybody trump like an elephant.
Bah like a sheep in a pen.

Piperoo says nay like a horse does.
Piperoo says ribbit like a frog.
Piperoo says meow like a pussy cat.
Piperoo says bark like a dog.
Piperoo says dance like an ape does.
Piperoo says jump like a flea.
Open your mouth like a crocodile.
Piperoo says buzz like a bee.

Piperoo says roar like a lion.
And squeak like a mouse does too.
Piperoo says moo like a cow does.
Then leap like a kangaroo.
Piperoo says squawk like a parrot

Piperoo says clap like a seal.
Piperoo says chatter like a dolphin.
Piperoo says slither like an eel.

Make the noises just one more.
Try them louder than before.
Piperoo says gulp like a goldfish.
Piperoo says hiss like a snake.
Piperoo says growl like a tiger.
Blow bubbles like a fish in a lake.
Piperoo says snort like a piggy.
Piperoo says cluck like a hen.
Everybody trump like an elephant.
Bah like a sheep in a pen.

Printed in Great Britain
by Amazon